WISDOM PRINCIPLES
FOR SUCCESS

"Timeless Strategies for Achieving Your Goals and Fulfilling Your Dreams"

OSCAR SYLVAN

Table of Contents

Table of Contents

Introduction

The Role of Wisdom in Achieving Success

In the grand tapestry of human existence, there exists an ever-persistent quest—a quest for success, for fulfillment, for a life of purpose and meaning. It is a journey that each of us embarks upon, a journey that spans across the vast landscapes of dreams and ambitions. Yet, in this quest, success remains an enigmatic and elusive destination, often shrouded in uncertainty and accompanied by a multitude of questions.

Wisdom is often regarded as the cornerstone of success, a timeless and invaluable principle that guides individuals toward achieving their goals and aspirations. In the journey to success, knowledge, and intelligence are undoubtedly important, but it is the application of wisdom that truly sets the stage for remarkable achievements. Wisdom encompasses not only the ability to accumulate and apply knowledge but also the discernment to make sound decisions, the patience to persevere through challenges, and the humility to learn from failures. In this exploration of the wisdom principle for success, we will delve into the profound ways in

which wisdom shapes our paths, empowers our choices, and ultimately leads us toward the fulfillment of our dreams and ambitions.

What is the key to achieving success? Is it intelligence, hard work, or perhaps sheer luck? While these factors undoubtedly play a significant role, there is another, often underestimated, and yet profoundly influential element that guides our steps on this journey: wisdom.

Wisdom, in its essence, represents the culmination of knowledge, experience, discernment, and insight. It is the art of making sound decisions, the ability to navigate the complexities of life with grace, and the capacity to learn from both triumphs and tribulations. In the context of our pursuit of success, wisdom is not merely a desirable trait; it is the linchpin, the secret ingredient that elevates us beyond the ordinary and propels us toward extraordinary achievements.

This book is an exploration of the wisdom principle for success—a principle that transcends the boundaries of time and culture, offering timeless guidance to those who seek it. It delves into the profound ways in which wisdom shapes our paths, empowers our choices, and ultimately leads us toward the fulfillment of our dreams and aspirations.

In the pages that follow, we will embark on a journey to unravel the mysteries of wisdom and success. We will learn how to define our purpose with unwavering clarity, make decisions that resonate with our deepest values, and cultivate the resilience to persevere through life's challenges. We will uncover the wisdom that can be gleaned from failure, the transformative power of humility, and the significance of building meaningful relationships along the way.

Moreover, we will explore how wisdom plays a pivotal role in leadership, not just in our professional lives but in the way we lead ourselves toward a life of significance. As we progress through these pages, we will reflect on the delicate balance between wisdom and ambition, understanding that true success is not measured solely by external achievements but by the fulfillment we find in the journey itself.

Dear reader, as you embark on this exploration of the wisdom principle for success, I invite you to open your heart and mind to the timeless insights that lie ahead. Together, let us unravel the profound relationship between wisdom and success, and in doing so, let us discover the keys to unlocking our full potential and realizing the aspirations that define our unique paths. The journey begins now, with the wisdom that has guided countless souls before us, and it is my sincere hope that it will illuminate the way forward on your quest for success.

Chapter 1

The Essence of Wisdom

Understanding Wisdom and Its Significance

Wisdom, that elusive quality revered across cultures and generations, is the subject of our first exploration. To truly harness its power in the pursuit of success, we must first grasp its essence. In this section, we delve into the multifaceted nature of wisdom, dissecting its components and discerning how it differs from knowledge and intelligence. We embark on a journey to understand the essence of wisdom and why it holds a pivotal place in the art of living a fulfilling and successful life.

The Relationship Between Wisdom and Success

Wisdom and success share an intricate and symbiotic relationship. While success often stands as the ultimate goal, wisdom serves as the compass that guides us toward it. In this part of the chapter, we explore the profound ways in which wisdom and success intertwine. We will uncover how wisdom influences our choices, decisions, and actions, ultimately shaping the path to success. Through real-life examples and anecdotes, we'll see how individuals who have achieved remarkable success have often been guided by their wisdom.

The Wisdom-Intelligence Distinction

Wisdom, intelligence, and knowledge are often used interchangeably, but they are distinct facets of human cognition. In this section, we make a clear distinction between wisdom and intelligence. We delve into the realms of intellect, explaining how intelligence relates to problem-solving and analytical skills, while wisdom encompasses a broader spectrum of human understanding, including empathy, compassion, and the ability to make ethical decisions. By understanding this distinction, we lay the foundation for recognizing and nurturing wisdom as an essential component of personal and professional success.

As we embark on this journey through the essence of wisdom, we invite you to reflect on your own experiences and insights, as well as those of wise individuals who have left their mark on the world. Have a deeper appreciation for the role of wisdom in your life and a clearer understanding of how it can lead you toward a more fulfilling and successful path.

The Process of Identifying, Refining, and Setting Your Definite Chief Aim

Your Definite Chief Aim is the central purpose or mission that directs your life's journey. It is the beacon that guides your actions, decisions, and aspirations. Identifying, refining, and setting your Definite Chief Aim is a process that requires deep self-reflection, clarity of purpose, and a commitment to aligning your life with your core values and passions.

Identifying Your Definite Chief Aim

Self-Exploration: Begin by exploring your life's experiences, interests, and values. What activities or pursuits have brought you the most joy, fulfillment, and a sense of purpose? Reflect on moments when you felt most aligned with your true self.

Values Assessment: Identify your core values. These are the principles that define what matters most to you. Your Definite Chief Aim should align with and reflect these values. Consider what principles guide your decisions and actions.

Passion Discovery: Delve into your passions and interests. What topics or activities excite you and make you feel alive? Passion is a powerful driving force that can fuel your pursuit of your Definite Chief Aim.

Refining Your Definite Chief Aim

Clarity and Specificity: Your Definite Chief Aim should be clear and specific. Avoid vague or general statements. Instead, articulate a precise mission or goal that reflects your deepest aspirations.

Alignment with Values: Ensure that your Definite Chief Aim is in alignment with your core values. It should feel congruent with your principles and beliefs, reflecting what you stand for.

Passion Integration: Infuse your passion into your Definite Chief Aim. Your pursuit should be something that genuinely excites and motivates you. Passion provides the energy and enthusiasm needed to persevere in the face of challenges.

Setting Your Definite Chief Aim

Write It Down: Transform your refined Definite Chief Aim into a written statement. This statement should be clear, concise, and inspiring. Write it in the present tense, as if it's already a reality.

Visualization: Create a mental image of your Definite Chief Aim. Visualize what achieving it looks and feels like. This visualization reinforces your commitment and helps you stay focused.

Affirmation: Develop a daily affirmation based on your Definite Chief Aim. Repeating this affirmation reinforces your belief in your mission and keeps it at the forefront of your mind.

The Importance of Aligning with Values and Passions

Aligning your Definite Chief Aim with your values and passions is crucial for several reasons:

Intrinsic Motivation: When your aim resonates with your values and passions, you are naturally more motivated to pursue it. It becomes a labor of love, not just a duty.

Sustainability: A Definite Chief Aim that aligns with your values and passions is more likely to endure over time. You'll be willing to invest the sustained effort required to achieve it.

Fulfillment: Living a life in alignment with your values and passions is inherently fulfilling. Your pursuit becomes an expression of your true self, leading to a deeper sense of purpose and contentment.

The Role of Wisdom in Staying True to Your Core Principles

Wisdom plays a pivotal role in ensuring that your pursuit remains true to your core principles. Wisdom involves discernment, perspective, and the ability to make sound judgments. Here's how wisdom contributes:

Balanced Decision-Making: Wisdom helps you make balanced decisions that consider not only your immediate desires but also the long-term consequences of your actions.

Adaptability: Wisdom allows you to adapt your pursuit as circumstances change without compromising your core principles. It helps you navigate challenges with grace and resilience.

Ethical Compass: Wisdom guides you in maintaining ethical integrity in the pursuit of your Definite Chief Aim. It prevents you from compromising your values for short-term gains.

In essence, wisdom is the rudder that steers your ship on the journey toward your Definite Chief Aim, ensuring that you stay true to your core principles and values along the way. It is the guardian of your mission, helping you make decisions that are not only purposeful but also aligned with your deepest beliefs and passions.

In conclusion, identifying, refining, and setting your Definite Chief Aim is a profound process that requires self-awareness, clarity, and alignment with your values and passions. When you infuse your pursuit with wisdom, you ensure that your journey remains true to your core principles, guiding you toward a life of meaningful purpose and fulfillment.

Chapter 2

Defining Your Definite Chief Aim

In the pursuit of success through the wisdom principle, it is essential to start with a clear and well-defined objective, often referred to as your "Definite Chief Aim." Your Definite Chief Aim is the North Star that guides your actions, decisions, and endeavors. It serves as the focal point around which your pursuit of wisdom revolves, ensuring that your journey is purposeful and directed.

Your Definite Chief Aim encapsulates your ultimate goal, the realization of your deepest desires, and the embodiment of your vision of success. It is not merely a fleeting wish but a meticulously crafted, unwavering aspiration that fuels your commitment to wisdom-driven actions. Crafting a Definite Chief Aim requires introspection, self-awareness, and a profound understanding of what you truly desire in life.

As we explore this chapter, we will delve into the process of identifying, refining and setting your Definite Chief Aim. We will discuss the importance of aligning your aim with your values and passions, and how wisdom plays a pivotal role in ensuring that your pursuit remains true to your core principles.

Moreover, we will examine real-life examples of individuals who have harnessed the wisdom principle to define their Definite Chief Aims and have subsequently achieved remarkable success. From business magnates to spiritual leaders, their journeys will inspire and provide valuable insights into the transformative power of a well-defined aim fueled by wisdom.

So, as we embark on this chapter, prepare to embark on a journey of self-discovery and purposeful planning. By the end, you will not only have a clear understanding of your Definite Chief Aim but also the wisdom-driven tools and strategies to navigate the path toward its realization.

Crafting a Clear and Inspiring Purpose

In the pursuit of success, a well-defined purpose serves as your guiding star. In this section, we will explore the art of crafting a Definite Chief Aim—a purpose that resonates deep within your soul. We'll delve into the significance of having a clear and inspiring aim, one that ignites your passion and provides direction in your life's journey. Through practical exercises and thought-provoking insights, you will learn how to articulate a purpose that motivates and empowers you to pursue your dreams relentlessly.

The Power of Clarity in Goal Setting

Clarity is the foundation upon which all great achievements are built. Here, we'll discuss the pivotal role that clarity plays in goal setting and achievement. You'll discover how to transform vague aspirations into tangible, well-defined goals that propel you forward. We'll explore techniques for breaking down complex objectives into manageable steps, enabling you to navigate your path with confidence and purpose. By the end of this section, you'll have the tools to set clear and actionable goals aligned with your Definite Chief Aim.

Aligning Your Aims with Your Values

Success that is meaningful and fulfilling stems from aligning your aims with your core values. In this section, we'll delve into the importance of values-based goal setting. You'll learn how to identify your values, the principles that guide your life, and how to ensure your Definite Chief Aim is in harmony with these values. By achieving this alignment, you not only increase your chances of success but also find a deeper sense of purpose and satisfaction in your pursuits.

This Chapter is your guide to defining your Definite Chief Aim—a purpose that will drive you forward on your journey to success. Through the power of clarity in goal setting and alignment with your core values, you'll embark on a path that resonates with your heart and soul, ensuring that your pursuit of success is not just about reaching the destination but also about enjoying the journey.

Chapter 3

Decision-Making and Discernment

The Art of Wise Decision-Making

Decision-making is an integral part of our daily lives, and it plays a pivotal role in the pursuit of success. In this section, we will explore the art of making decisions wisely. You'll gain insights into the factors that influence our choices and the strategies to make informed, well-considered decisions. We'll delve into the importance of balancing intuition, rationality, and emotional intelligence in the decision-making process. By mastering the art of wise decision-making, you'll empower yourself to navigate the complexities of your journey with confidence.

Learning from Past Choices

Our past choices, both successes and failures, hold valuable lessons that can guide us toward greater wisdom and success in the future. In this section, we'll discuss the transformative power of learning from past choices. You'll explore techniques for reflection and self-evaluation, allowing you to extract wisdom from your experiences. By understanding the impact of your decisions and adapting based on lessons learned, you'll enhance your ability to make sound choices on your path to success.

Cultivating Discernment in Everyday Life

Discernment is the ability to distinguish between right and wrong, truth and falsehood, and wise and unwise choices. In this section, we'll delve into the process of cultivating discernment in your everyday life. You'll learn to sharpen your judgment, develop a keen sense of intuition, and become more attuned to the subtle nuances that influence your decisions. By honing your discernment skills, you'll be better equipped to navigate the challenges and opportunities that arise, ensuring that your choices align with your pursuit of success.

This is your guide to mastering the art of decision-making and cultivating discernment—a vital component of the wisdom principle for success. By making wise choices, learning from your experiences, and developing discernment in your daily life, you'll enhance your ability to chart a course toward success that is characterized by clarity, intentionality, and wisdom.

Chapter 4

Perseverance and Patience

The Virtue of Patience on the Road to Success

In the fast-paced world of instant gratification, patience is often overlooked, yet it stands as a fundamental virtue on the journey to success. In this section, we will explore the profound significance of patience in achieving your goals. You'll gain insights into the power of delayed gratification, the ability to weather storms with equanimity, and the role of patience in maintaining long-term focus. By embracing patience as a guiding virtue, you'll be better prepared to navigate the challenges that inevitably arise on your path to success.

Overcoming Obstacles with Perseverance

Obstacles are an inevitable part of any worthwhile journey, and perseverance is the key to surmounting them. In this section, we'll delve into the art of perseverance—the unwavering determination to press on in the face of adversity. You'll explore real-life stories of individuals who overcame seemingly insurmountable obstacles through sheer grit and resilience. By understanding the importance of perseverance, you'll discover how setbacks can become stepping stones on your path to success.

Balancing Patience and Productivity

Balancing patience with productivity is an art that requires finesse. In this section, we'll discuss how to strike the right balance between patiently waiting for the fruits of your labor and taking decisive, action-oriented steps toward your goals. You'll learn practical strategies for managing your time, setting realistic expectations, and avoiding the pitfalls of impatience. By achieving this balance, you'll enhance your effectiveness in working towards your vision of success.

Chapter 4 is your guide to embracing the virtues of perseverance and patience on your journey to success. By recognizing the profound significance of patience, learning to overcome obstacles with unwavering determination, and striking the right balance between patience and productivity, you'll fortify your resilience and enhance your ability to achieve your long-cherished aspirations.

Chapter 5

Learning from Failure

Embracing Failure as a Source of Wisdom

Failure, often feared and avoided, is a powerful teacher on the journey to success. In this section, we will explore the transformative practice of embracing failure as a source of wisdom. You'll gain insights into reframing failure as an opportunity for growth and learning. We'll discuss the psychological resilience required to face failure head-on and the wisdom that can be gleaned from these challenging experiences. By adopting a new perspective on failure, you'll open the door to profound personal and professional development.

Extracting Lessons from Setbacks

Setbacks and disappointments are an inevitable part of any ambitious endeavor. In this section, we'll delve into the process of extracting valuable lessons from setbacks. You'll learn techniques for introspection and self-analysis, enabling you to uncover the hidden gems of wisdom within moments of adversity. By understanding the root causes of setbacks and failures, you'll be better equipped to adjust your strategies and continue progressing toward your goals.

Using Failure as a Stepping Stone to Success

Failure need not be a dead-end but rather a stepping stone on the path to success. In this section, we'll discuss how to harness the wisdom gained from failure to propel you forward. You'll explore inspiring stories of individuals who turned their failures into catalysts for extraordinary success. By applying the lessons learned from setbacks, you'll find the resilience and determination to rise above challenges and move closer to your vision of success.

Chapter 5 is your guide to navigating the inevitable setbacks and failures that accompany the pursuit of success. By embracing failure as a source of wisdom, extracting valuable lessons from setbacks, and using those experiences as stepping stones, you'll not only bounce back from adversity but also accelerate your progress toward the achievement of your goals.

Chapter 6

Humility and Lifelong Learning

The Role of Humility in Wisdom

Humility, often regarded as a hallmark of wisdom, has a profound impact on our personal and professional growth. In this section, we will explore the significance of humility in the pursuit of wisdom. You'll gain a deeper understanding of how humility fosters open-mindedness, empathy, and a willingness to learn from others. We'll delve into real-life examples of humble leaders and thinkers who have left an indelible mark on history. By appreciating the role of humility, you'll cultivate a mindset that is receptive to the wisdom of others and open to personal growth.

The Growth Mindset and Continuous Learning

A growth mindset, characterized by the belief that abilities and intelligence can be developed through dedication and hard work, is a key element of lifelong learning. In this section, we'll discuss the concept of a growth mindset and its role in fostering continuous learning. You'll explore strategies for adopting and maintaining a growth mindset, allowing you to embrace challenges and setbacks as opportunities for development. By cultivating this mindset, you'll empower yourself to continually acquire new knowledge and skills on your journey to success.

Seeking Wisdom from Diverse Sources

Wisdom can be found in a myriad of places and perspectives. In this section, we'll delve into the practice of seeking wisdom from diverse sources. You'll learn how to expand your horizons by engaging with people from various backgrounds, cultures, and experiences. We'll explore the importance of listening actively and empathetically to others' viewpoints. By broadening your sources of wisdom, you'll enrich your understanding of the world and gain insights that can enhance your decision-making and problem-solving abilities.

This Chapter serves as a guide to the transformative power of humility and lifelong learning. By recognizing the role of humility in wisdom, adopting a growth mindset for continuous learning, and seeking wisdom from diverse sources, you'll cultivate a mindset and approach to life that not only enriches your journey but also contributes to the collective wisdom of humanity.

Chapter 7

Building Meaningful Relationships

Nurturing Wise and Supportive Connections

Meaningful relationships are not just essential for personal well-being; they also play a pivotal role in the pursuit of success. In this section, we will explore the art of nurturing wise and supportive connections. You'll learn how to identify and cultivate relationships that align with your values and goals. We'll discuss the importance of trust, empathy, and effective communication in building meaningful connections that can provide guidance and support on your journey.

Collaborative Wisdom in Success

Success is often a collective endeavor and collaboration with others can be a wellspring of wisdom. In this section, we'll delve into the concept of collaborative wisdom. You'll discover how diverse perspectives and expertise can lead to innovative solutions and better decision-making. We'll explore case studies and real-world examples of how collaborative wisdom has propelled individuals and organizations to achieve remarkable success. By harnessing the power of collaboration, you can tap into a collective pool of knowledge and experience that accelerates your path to success.

The Wisdom of Emotional Intelligence

Emotional intelligence, the ability to recognize and manage your own emotions and those of others, is a critical component of building meaningful relationships and achieving success. In this section, we'll discuss the wisdom of emotional intelligence. You'll learn how emotional intelligence enhances your ability to navigate interpersonal dynamics, resolve conflicts, and build rapport. We'll provide practical strategies for developing emotional intelligence skills that can strengthen your relationships and contribute to your overall success.

Chapter 7 serves as your guide to understanding the profound impact of meaningful relationships on the wisdom principle for success. By nurturing wise and supportive connections, embracing collaborative wisdom, and developing emotional intelligence, you'll not only enrich your personal and professional life but also tap into a valuable resource that can enhance your journey toward success.

Chapter 8

Leading with Wisdom

Wisdom in Leadership Roles

In the realm of leadership, wisdom emerges as a defining trait that distinguishes exceptional leaders from the rest. This chapter delves deep into the concept of wisdom in leadership, exploring how it transforms ordinary managers into visionary guides who inspire and empower their teams. Leadership is not just about making decisions; it's about making wise decisions that resonate with the greater good. We'll examine the key attributes of wise leaders, from their ability to see the bigger picture to their knack for fostering a culture of trust and collaboration within their organizations.

Inspiring Others through Wise Leadership

Wise leadership extends beyond making sound choices; it's about inspiring others to join you on the journey toward a shared vision. In this section, we'll explore the art of inspiring and motivating individuals through wisdom-driven leadership. We'll discuss how wisdom enhances a leader's emotional intelligence, allowing them to connect with their teams on a deeper level. Additionally, we'll delve into the power of storytelling, ethical decision-making, and empathetic communication as essential tools for wise leaders who seek to ignite passion and commitment among their followers.

Case Studies in Wise Leadership

The wisdom principle in leadership comes to life through real-world examples of individuals who have left an indelible mark on their organizations, communities, and the world at large. In this chapter, we will dissect case studies of renowned leaders who have harnessed the power of wisdom to navigate complex challenges, foster innovation, and drive meaningful change. From historical figures like Mahatma Gandhi and Nelson Mandela to contemporary business leaders who have transformed their companies, these case studies serve as beacons of inspiration, illustrating the tangible outcomes that can be achieved through wise leadership.

As we explore wisdom in leadership, we aim to equip you with the knowledge, skills, and insights needed to become a wise and impactful leader in your own right. Whether you're leading a team, a company, or a community, the principles and stories shared in this chapter will illuminate the path to becoming a beacon of wisdom, guiding those around you toward success, growth, and fulfillment.

Chapter 9

Balancing Wisdom with Ambition

Striking a Balance Between Wisdom and Drive

In the pursuit of success, ambition can be a powerful driving force, propelling individuals to achieve their goals and dreams. However, when ambition is not tempered by wisdom, it can lead to reckless decision-making and unintended consequences. In this chapter, we will explore the delicate art of striking a balance between wisdom and ambition. We will delve into how wisdom can guide and harness ambition, ensuring that your aspirations are pursued with a clear sense of purpose and long-term vision.

Avoiding Pitfalls of Impulsive Ambition

Impulsive ambition can be a double-edged sword, capable of both propelling individuals forward and causing them to stumble. We will examine the common pitfalls associated with impulsive ambition and how they can be avoided through the application of wisdom. From hasty decision-making to neglecting self-care, we will provide practical strategies for mitigating the negative consequences of unchecked ambition and steering your journey toward a more deliberate and fulfilling path.

Sustainable Success through Wise Ambition

Sustainable success is not merely about achieving short-term goals; it is about building a legacy that endures over time. We will explore how wise ambition is intrinsically tied to sustainable success, allowing individuals to navigate the ever-changing landscape of their ambitions while maintaining a sense of purpose and ethical integrity. Through real-world examples and expert insights, we will showcase the profound impact of wise ambition on long-lasting achievements and personal fulfillment.

This will help you have a comprehensive understanding of how wisdom can serve as a guiding force in balancing ambition, enabling you to pursue your dreams with clarity, resilience, and a commitment to lasting success.

Chapter 10

Cultivating a Life of Fulfillment

The Ultimate Reward: A Fulfilling Life

In the pursuit of success, the ultimate goal for many is not just material wealth or recognition but a life filled with profound meaning and fulfillment. This chapter explores the concept of fulfillment as the ultimate reward of a life well-lived. We will delve into the importance of aligning one's actions, ambitions, and values to create a life that brings a deep sense of contentment and purpose. Through inspiring stories and practical guidance, you will discover how wisdom plays a pivotal role in unlocking the door to a truly fulfilling existence.

Balancing Success with Well-Being

Achieving success is a worthy pursuit, but it should never come at the expense of one's well-being. In this section, we will explore the crucial balance between success and well-being, emphasizing the wisdom required to prioritize physical, mental, and emotional health. We will provide strategies for avoiding burnout, maintaining work-life balance, and nurturing personal relationships—all while striving for success. Ultimately, you will learn how wisdom can help you create a harmonious life where success and well-being coexist.

Leaving a Legacy of Wisdom

As we conclude our journey through the wisdom principle for success, we turn our attention to the legacy you leave behind. True fulfillment often comes from making a positive impact on others and the world. We will explore how wisdom-driven success can lead to the creation of a lasting legacy of wisdom, inspiring future generations to follow in your footsteps. Whether through mentorship, philanthropy, or the dissemination of knowledge, this chapter will guide you in crafting a legacy that reflects the wisdom you've cultivated and the success you've achieved.

By now, you would have gained a comprehensive understanding of how wisdom can transform your pursuit of success into a lifelong journey of fulfillment. You will be equipped with the knowledge and tools to maintain balance, well-being, and the capacity to make a meaningful impact, leaving behind a legacy that embodies the principles of wisdom and success.

Conclusion

The Endless Journey of Wisdom and Success

In the culmination of our exploration into the profound interplay between wisdom and success, we find ourselves at the threshold of an endless journey—a journey characterized by growth, learning, and continuous evolution. The wisdom principle, as we have come to understand, is not a destination but a lifelong companion that guides our steps on the path to success and fulfillment.

Throughout this journey, we have uncovered the fundamental role of wisdom in shaping our decisions, our actions, and ultimately, our destinies. We have seen how wisdom serves as a steady hand that steadies us through the storms of uncertainty, as a beacon of light that illuminates the darkest of moments, and as a wellspring of resilience that fuels our determination in the face of adversity.

We have learned that wisdom is not the exclusive domain of the elderly or the erudite; it is a resource accessible to all who seek it. It is a quality that can be cultivated and refined, and a principle that can be integrated into every facet of our lives, from our personal relationships to our professional pursuits.

Our journey has taken us through the intricacies of defining a Definite Chief Aim, leading with wisdom, balancing ambition, and ultimately, cultivating a life of fulfillment. We have witnessed the transformative power of wisdom in the lives of individuals and the collective progress of societies. We have seen how wisdom serves as the cornerstone upon which enduring success is built, and how it imbues our achievements with a profound sense of purpose.

As we conclude our exploration, let us remember that the journey of wisdom and success is an ongoing, ever-rewarding endeavor. It is a journey that invites us to remain open to new experiences, to continually seek knowledge, and to adapt and refine our understanding of wisdom as we evolve. It is a journey that acknowledges that setbacks and challenges are integral parts of the path, each offering valuable lessons that contribute to our growth.

In the end, the wisdom principle reminds us that success is not a finite destination but a dynamic, ever-evolving process. It beckons us to embrace the endless journey with an open heart and a steadfast commitment to wisdom, knowing that as we do, the possibilities for personal growth, fulfillment, and the betterment of the world are truly limitless.